For Jacal — chor dancer, oft and laughter when needed. Best, Phyllis

SHOVELER
ON THE ROOF

Selected Poems
by Phyllis Rachel Larrabee

Cover Art and Illustrations by
E. G. "Peskunck" Larrabee

i

Works
By Phyllis Rachel Larrabee

Poetry Books

Old Leaflets for Shopping Lists
and Rashly Written Poems
Cream of Red Pepper
Road to Alachua
P'towbuk
We had Trouble Getting to
Chetamol
Careful of the Cosmos
Complaints in Paradise
Edges of the Moon
Official Spring
Shorter Days, Longer Nights
Lucky Garden
Pipsiwas/Firefly
Plenty of Summer Left
Sol-Sticks
Shoveler on the Roof

Plays

The Alley
Love, Medicine and Mishugas

   with Malcolm E. Sawyer
Startruck
Tagadozik/Strike: The Anti-War
Anti-Planetary-Devastation
Musical

To my husband
for all the men he can be.

With great thanks to family and friends for listening and love, for giving me seed money, equipment and time and for lending me faith.

Shoveler on the Roof

Printed by L. Brown & Sons Printing, Inc.
14 Jefferson St.
Barre, Vermont 05641

Cover Art and Illustrations by
E. G. "Peskunck" Larrabee

ISBN 0-9787645-0-1

Printed in the United States
of America

Contents

Plenty of Summer Left

Shorter Days, Longer Nights

Shorter Days, Longer Nights (continued)

Shoveler on the Roof

Mud Season & Spring

Plenty of
Summer Left

Green Birch

green birch
   green popular
      green ash
white pine

         circle the pond in a daze

i'm just one of the tadpoles
            wriggling
around
     and drinking the water
    like creme de menthe.

Bugs' Flute

The bugs whistle
through the hollows
flutes of labor.

a satyr swings me
down a path
of weeds and ferns
and grasses --
tickling
till the first yarrow

where a fat amber worm
sits on white blossoms
& orders

--"Don't upset me
   from my perch!"

but I'm just
phyllis in wonderland
ambling
to the upper meadows.

I Looked for You in Fields
of Unsettled Stone

i looked for you in fields
of unsettled stone
with raised welts
of nettles
stinging arms and legs
                              teased
by blue
    and purple thistles
by complaints
of sheep

to say:
this is another country.

beyond the pungent cries
of catnip
in your arms
the pennyroyal hides
tiny but not frail

holding on
in crevices of rocks
and where ancient fences crackle.

Sweet Nervine

with eyes
of sun-green chamomile
   sweet nervine

child

elf

man

you hold me
   in shadows
                   of forgotten
covers

brewing
   with me
sarsaparilla wine

     from almost
        chocolate roots.

Sharper than Light

sharper
> than light

through flickering
> leaves

the saw grunts
> at the wood

pierces
> the day.

sweat rains
on the valiant

subsisting
> on cheese

and potato chips

cutting their cords
> in threatened woods.

Sunborn Diamonds

Sunborn diamonds
glitter
on the water.

A heron takes off
and flies East.

And in the
distance

                paddles of
                a kayak

dart in
and out
of the water

silver spangled
by the
morning's light.

Edges of the Moon

Above the leaves soaking up
thin dew
the edges of the moon define
its reluctance
to fade from the morning sky.

Clammy in my suit
I slump down the stairs
surprised to see
how the mist fattens above the
waters to the opposite shore
each day a little more

shrouds the trees on that shore
so they bleed into each other
like watercolors
hiding my neighbors
barking to their dog.

I peel off my suit.

No one but the raven would notice
only water striders will witness
the lovemaking
between
the skin of warm water and mine.

Juno

Gold threads
  weaving under blue waves
where bass mimic silk
  swishing through shadows
and arms weave strokes above
  solar so-lit waters.

Gold threads
 wedging in the Earth
brewing medicine unseen
 where moss runs the hills
caresses feet green

invites white berry blossoms
to share the terrain
as polka dots
as stars
opening everywhere
to love
and
rain.

Breakfast

Are those ducks squabbling
at breakfast unseen
while sunlight scatters a thousand
shining coins in the center
of the lake?

Yes.

The lake allows the mist
letting go
while boats rest in dock
loyal as dogs.

A door slams
then quiet
and I can no longer ignore
their dance

the dance of a hundred
water striders
weaving in front of our dock

inviting me
irresistibly
to their morning Tai-chi.

Echo of Kyoto

Ky o to
sounds like a key
to fresh air

a late dream of
corporate responsibility
bringing yesterday's paper outside
where fish leap in the air
and the wood thrush
sings: WE can't wait!

I go down to the lake
to its burka of mist
eyeing the heron
gracefully plowing through the air
blue against gray morning

while around me
dandelion greens and plantain
and orange paintbrush blossoms
wake up, shake off their shower
and loons wail
and bull frogs thrum
and the morning dove
well...mourns

and I hear the call
of a thousand strawberries
to touch summer to my teeth.

Transplanting

Awake before the black flies
Wigwe-dzize-gibsak

I transplant dark Earth
from our woods
to the pale dust of my garden
and transplant lush delicata
and buttercup and pumpkin
to hills already holding
their sister corn.
              I settle in the fragrant
green basil, so ready to roost

Near noon they all look
as wilted as I feel.
I water them some more.

Will water do it for me? Maybe.
The news at noon reports
our government may
resort to force
if the North Koreans
don't give up the development
of nuclear arms.

In addressing himself to the
Palestinian people, our President
says: "If you keep up the
violence, you'll get...nothin'."

What Wakes me?

What wakes me?

The loon calls   mda-hila
                  magic bird
black flies, too. wigwe-dzize-
gibsak.

I dress accordingly
no accordion- pleated skirt!
pulling on padded jeans
to avoid insect bites
adding my head net
my long white shirt
and jacket and
so slowly
shhh-ing down to the lake

to chant the Shma
to sing the oneness
of all creation.

The loon flies
over the water
to look at this creature, me
in black and white.

Hey, big sister, what are you?
I keep chanting
and the loon flies away, trilling.

Reflecting

Walking through garden
with granddaughter
'round the sunflowers
tomatoes and
lemon basil
we approach tall pink
and purple blossoms:
my wedding bouquet.

"Be careful of the cosmos,"
I tell her.

Then rain falls
and I take her hand
run towards the house
laughing.

She stops me.
"Wait," she says.

"What?"

"Be careful of the cosmos."

Rice Milk Mist

Rice milk mist drapes
itself over the lake
tempts me down
the strawberry path
to the water.

Now, the mist parts
in frayed cheesecloth threads
and what is left?

A heron
standing on a dock
near the opposite shore.

I slip off my clothes
and walk in
carry no stones.

Walk into the quiet
just the water
and the heron
and the silver moon setting
in the rose quartz sky.

And even after I splash
and splash noisily
the heron stands still waiting,
The heron waits.

Last Night

Last night
the lake dreamt
of a silver shark

one of the 375 kinds of sharks
peaceful
to man and woman and child.

Sharks so mild!

In the early morning
only the skin of the shark
remains
floating on the surface

(and did the shark dream of
375 kinds of man, woman and
child peaceful t'sharks?).

Father Loon

Father loon has gone belly up
his white underside
gleaming in the waters
his shining batik designs
of black and white
      close enough
                for me to shoot
a picture.
Crouched behind the
blueberry bush
I know I am seen.
I cannot shoot even a picture
but hold my breath
then breathe in awe
at this diversion.
                So this is
what is meant
by a diversion.
He risks his beauty, his life
before this stranger, me
         as his child
        the furry chick
       swims off with mom
to the middle of the lake

and in silence
I sign: understanding
his risking everything for his child
my heart
drumming to his.

Heavy Dew

Carefully
I close the door
to your room
upon myself

open myself
to a crystal garden
yawning with lilies.

Who has made this morning
dew white as milk
brushing the grass with silk?

Who has made this morning
polishing the milkweed
hardy, iridescent and blue?

Who has made this morning
but me and you
making love
making dew

the secret of a summer
green without rain.

Dusk Ride

Black cattle munch
on lush grass
green

where the skies give up
their light

polishing the hills copper
before pink clouds
before the night.

And I notice
driving to the store
for fish, cucumbers
and bread

then returning home
along a quiet road
groceries tucked in
the cooler, in the car

I notice
a pear sliver of moon
appear like a ghost to the
tune of radio's "Blue Moon."

"Now, I'm no longer alone."

After the Full Moon

After the full moon
two purple petunias are left
their sisters gone.

I stand by the petunias
and a grasshopper stops me cold
so gold and green
hopping away fast as the crickets'
song.

What's remaining?

the red and rose of bee balm

the corn

and all the gold blossoms
of squash
like stars
falling to the ground

but holding the promise

of real pie

on

Earth.

North Country Thrift

In the company
of green pumpkins
and tall, thin corn

I listen to the crickets' August
band
wrapped in the stillness of trees
against a bearskin sky
with one peeking star.

Somewhere
raccoons wait
for me to disappear

but I slouch on the porch
kidnapped
by the hidden moon

can't resist
sucking all the summer
from the night's bones.

Tallit

The mist like a tallit
wraps the hill
still at mid morning
each day
darker   cooler
we crave more covers
more light
notice how leafy
is the siddur   always

and the maples and birch are leafy
mostly green
while the hills rust at the edges.

a gold leaf
falls into the water. Ouch.

but turning to the shores
you can see light

where bouquets of purple aster
linger   not yet frosted
nor blown away
spring up from the Earth
and sway with gold hearts
to purple the last days of summer.

Shorter Days,
Longer Nights

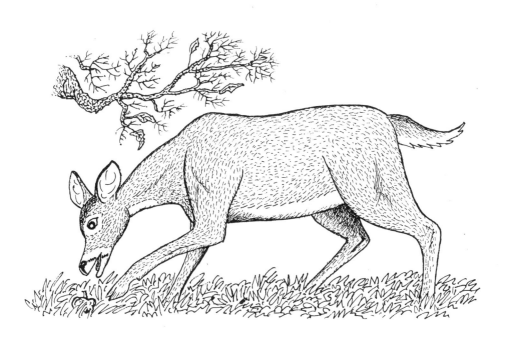

Before You Left

Before you left
you taught me the secrets
of apples at the foot
of the garden
and many other things

how the rain
paints the harvest
on mooncalf nights
gliding past
rushing stars.

Before you left
I could not find these words.

Is it possible
to walk gingerly in boots
on caked leaves

and when the coltsfoot
turns purple
will it still be good
for the pain in my chest?

Elul

Dark silk spun after sunset
spills onto the waters.

I watch light and darkness
scurrying to seek favor
to curry favor
with each other
with water
where quiet does not mean still.

And then
lights come on across the lake
spinning dervishes of gold
deep into the waves

a vision
tickling the night

resolutions
for the new moon.

Anniversary

For our anniversary morning
imagine love on soft, flannel
sheets and purple pillows.

Imagine an afternoon walk
blessing the woods
with our whispers celebrating
the path beneath our feet
collages of red and yellow leaves
and all colors in between

discovering tracks
of coyote and deer and where the
Earth turned black
velvet, wet, swampy
we turned back.

Sometimes, I hope to be
lost in the woods
and be unable to return
to civilization.

But that afternoon
two kangaroo ATVs charged past
kangaroo -- they had little seats
like pockets for little kids
and big seats for big guys
and the boys in helmets and dark
goggles and heavy jackets sat
armored against
the foot prints of the woods.

Feng-Shui

Two pine trees
stand in chill afternoon

encircled by leaves
red, pink, tangerine
yellow, brown, green

and mottled apples
cold and sweet
to the taste
fallen to the ground.

Eventually the deer will come
for the last apple
unburied by snow
and the garden
will become

bare of everything
but children's laughter

and needles
of
the evergreen.

Nava l'Ora Means I Have Beautiful Light

Baby Nava L'Ora sits in the
garden
of her mother's lap
but does not rest

her moon face
and earth brown eyes
and eager mouth
as round as the apple
she reaches for.

Her mother the rabbi
sunny and relaxed
on the brightest day
October can offer
takes an apple, too.

Blessed art thou
Source of Life
who brings forth
fruit from the trees.

And I am offered almonds
also the fruit of a tree.

Nava L'Ora bites past
red apple skin
relishes the white, sweet
grainy flesh and juice
of the apple.

She chews on
untainted by sugar or centuries
surrounded by the awe
of two women.

"She has only two teeth,"
her mother tells me.
Isn't that what courage is about?
Chewing with the teeth we have
and the teeth we dream of?

I'm dreaming too
of pink and white almond
blossoms after the long white
winter to come.

Nava L'Ora, you are still chewing
on that apple.
You have hollowed out
that apple almost to the core.

You are the new baby,
our new leader
as glorious as Gloria Steinem.

You thrive in the fragrant house
where no one thanks God for not
being born a woman.

Hallowe'en

Snow beads the windshield
hard as Hallowe'en candy
hard as hail.

I arrive at Hays Auto Repair.
Rewind
behind the windshield
to the breezes at the lake
where I chanted with the waves.

Now back to the garage...

I don't ask the mechanic
to come outside
while the snow falls.

Even with chemical
sensitivities
I drive into the garage   as if
hell were the only choice.
 The mechanic asks me
to lower the window
so I can hear him.   I do,
But his "emergency brake"
still sounds like "regency cake."

Nearby short and tall guys linger
hold lit cigarettes by their knees.
I hope we don't blow up.

My registration returned
my new sticker in place

I toss a check
to the mechanic   I   mean, toss!
and escape South.

Driving back to Hardwick
I listen to the radio
to tales and prophesies
of smallpox   and new
restrictions against immigrants.
No one wants terrorists
in their borders
but how would we know?
                I remember
                my love's T-shirt
            says 'INDIAN TIME'
            white background
            a picture framed in red:

English explorers, armed
meeting nine Native Americans
who offer fish and other gifts

but the questions
from the Indians:

"Illegal aliens
Who are they?
What do they want?"

Winter Wry

Snow laces the edges
of the garden

like sugar
dusting on broccoli
and lemon balm's
serrate leaves

snow on and off
the seed of winter rye.

Chocolate Earth
white snow.

Hydrox cookie colors
against the green spires
of spruce

and thin cold fingers
of maple and beech

offering alms
to the forever skies --

uneasy truce
before the morning news.

Don't Tread on Me

Cluster bombs
5,000 pound bombs
dropped
deluge Afghani
mothers, fathers, kids
wrapped in clothes
that can't keep out
wind or war.

Ain't that terror?

I drive home
warm in the dark.
My love drives home in the rain.

I hope he has his key.

The lights are on.
He is home.
              He brings
the flag into the house
his red-and-white striped
with-a-yellow-snake-
'DON'T TREAD ON ME' flag.
"Look!"

I look.

The stripes are bleeding.

A Butterfly

A butterfly alights
on a hemlock branch
where last night's snow
crunches under my feet.

Why are you here now,
butterfly?

Are you like me

doing your best

and still

you have not won

enough

frequent

flier

miles?

Snow Quilts

Snow quilts the fields satin
where threads of grass poke through
and Greenwood's lake shines
like tin
still flowing with the wind

and I remember
when I shiver

how watery
we are

and

kindle
not a candle

but a spring
       bubbling

in my autumn heart.

Soldiers Speak

At a small, blue shul
Yonatan Shapira, tanned and
earnest, reminds me of my
brother, Yuss, no longer with us,
tells the gantza m'gilla:
Why he won't obey illegal orders
to raid their homes, to drop bombs
on Palestinians: (The Israeli Air
Force threw him out.)

"Ask me your toughest
questions!" he says,
"What about the bombing of
Dresden?" someone asks (an
example to follow?)

"The Palestinians, like us, want to
be free.   We need to sweep our
side of the street. We need to be
tough lovers -- of Israel."

He hugs a soldier who says
he went to 16 funerals of his
comrades in two days and he
orders men under his command:
"Respect Palestinian farmers.
Respect the land."
"This man is a moral soldier,"
says Yonatan. "We have hope.
**We have to stop the cycle of
revenge -- so that we can live."**

36

Coming in to Puerto Penesco

Light blazes on the white
of the patio
where the ledge supports
seven gulls
politely watching us
savor our fish.

Below us
the sea heaves
against black rocks.

In a just world
the waitress
intelligent and elegant
would be
president or queen.

For now,
we flash smiles at her.
She beams.

exchange
Spanish for English
she, my son and I

while below us
the sea, catching the sun
light as crochet
heaves
against the rocks.

A Vigil

Twenty-nine women
stand in jackets of wind
and Michael joins them.

You can't keep a good man away
from the vigil of Women in Black.

Snow falls and roses bloom
on Lucy's black scarf.
She speaks to reporters:
"Stop the bombing so food and
medicine can get through."

Thirty people stand
wrapped in wind and flurries
and Chryss appears
unfurling a banner.

You can't keep a good man away
from the vigil of Women in Black.

The banner shows a blue planet
on it. Is that ours?
We claim Earth by being here.

"Can you help Ann hold up the
banner?"
"I'll only be here for ten minutes."
"Can you help me hold up the
world for ten minutes?" asks Ann.
"Yes."

Kitchen Mantra

The chalk board
on the window sill above the sink
gaily chanted
in purple, green, blue and white:
"What is the most loving action
I can take in this moment?"

The letters were close knit
ornamental and hard to read.

Through late spring,
summer, early autumn,
sometimes paper plates kept me
at a distance.

Sometimes
my hands in soapy water
scrubbing dishes, mugs
pots, forks, spoons, knives
I saw it, but didn't pay attention.
I knew the question was there
taken for granted like any old
jewel.

Just before the first snow
I turned the chalk board over.
Now it reads in pink and blue
letters:

"Keep Water Dripping."

Shoveler on
the Roof

On Our Roof

On our roof, our tapered roof
you shovel
I push the snow to the edge
turn it over and whack it off.
        Here I feel
closer to you
to the iced mountains
looming across the lake,
to the bare maples, beech
and green spruce
to swatches of blue
and drained clouds.

Eventually
my lungs marble with cold
and smoke from the chimney.
I'm ready to go down.

Stay a little longer, you urge me.
I do, keeping to the edge
digging out the roof's gutter
with a maple branch
till we hear the honking
and look up to
a hundred geese in a ragged V
chanting across the skies.

Exodus.

To an Onion at Winter Solstice

Who calls this a homely
vegetable?

Are the monks right to say it is
lascivious and ban it from their
homes in the Himalayas-- and the
yogis to banish it from their
kitchens in the Bahamas?

especially this red onion
its satin carmine covers
falling open to the next layer
of purple silk kissing scarlet skin

and then eight concentric layers
white but embroidered with
purple thread

and not quite in the middle
a shining egg-yolk light
surrounded by
a half circle of rose-tinted white
and above that half circle
a sister or lover shape
not quite half and
not quite pear
with another gold light
at its center
ready to leap
from there to here.

I Imagine You're a Catamount

I imagine you're a catamount
who has digested the last of his
deer

or a bear too deep
in winter sleep
to care.

I climb into bed
for mammal warmth
for your male animal warmth

and as my heart listens to yours
I smile giddily.

You are my mirror
you are my man

love in revival
you're my hero

of post-retirement
survival.

Putting Up the Bird Feeder

You were so tired
maybe with a touch of flu
and I said
I can't stand another winter
without chickadees
even if we feed the squirrels, too.

Okay, lets do it, you said
and I bought some suet.

Though the winds were mighty
howling as coyote
we went outside
you in your coonskin hat
making you look like
some tall, strange cat
and me in your red wool cap
and the red coat
patched with hearts
worn on the sleeves
and mismatched gloves.

We went out to the deep freeze.

You carried the feed and the bird
feeder & I carried the small
kitchen ladder.

And we went back to get a spool
of wire while afternoon shadows
grew longer
and I wished we were stronger
and longed to be close to a fire.

Your cheeks reddening
my hands the same
you put up the suet holder and
stuck in the pink meat
while the winds thrashed us
What a feat!

You stood on the ladder to
attach the bird feeder to the wire.

You perched precarious
an acrobat at a circus.

I handed you a cup and
we poured in the millet
and sunflower seeds
smiled/ finished
with our good deed

and walked inside
to defrost to the furnace's lullaby
and to read
Frost and Larrabee.

A DaVinci Tarot

In the co-op kitchen
Tina's black hair
cascades like satin
as she bends to cut
a purple cabbage in half.

She smiles
a full, quiet smile

like

like... Mona Lisa!

Was it so easy to guess

the why of the portrait's
happiness?

Tina is with child.

But, perhaps
Mona Lisa had just come up
with the formula
$E = mc^2$

and was keeping quiet
about it

because who would pay
attention to her anyway?

Pay attention
as Tina cuts the purple cabbage
in two

and a white goddess
is revealed.
"A white angel," she says.
(with eleven arms).

As if she were reading
Tarot cards or tea leaves

Tina has told her fortune

a mother to be
she may have to be
an angel with eleven arms.

Tu B'Shvat at a Yoga Center

The moon swells
towards fullness
pulling shadows
from the apple trees

till they stretch
across cold grass
shimmy like vines
up the walls
of the women's dorm.

It's just a phase
the moon will say

the light
not even mine
not even my own

but its fullness
will draw the blood
from women

and babies
from their wombs

and the trees will be
reborn.

Snow Dance at Mount Ascutney
Ski Resort

Here in a space station
built on skis
grandmother moon glares

while trunks of maple and birch
shiver
as the light and shadows of
unearthed ancestors' bones.

We, Wabanakiak
people of the morning light
have been called upon
to dance for snow.

We have been called
to undo the bad things done
to Earth and Air
with our dance.

The dance was laughed at
before.

"Dance!"
They told an old man.
Raymond Yellow Thunder
was his name.

"Dance!"
and shot him and stuffed him
in the trunk of a car.

Now the clouds are timid.
Lungs of the wind sputter
and cough.

Snow tucks us in
but the rain beats upon the snow
and the ice follows and chills.

Dreams tuck us in
but the rain beats upon our brow
and the ice -- like an axe --saws
and kills.

Last summer fried us
a warming trend.
The greenhouse effect
is the opposite of green.

And today in the sun
we will dance

where the mother mountain
has been captured with dollars
her head shaven in stripes
for the pleasure
of people from cities
where the snow-making machines
groan and whine

Here where the snow
which fell
like gold
does not fall
we will dance.

Says the earnest man
of Ascutney
                    all smiles and
charm.

"We welcome the Indians back
with open arms."

Crumbling

On the roof
the ice crumbles
beneath a metal shovel
& a plastic snow scoop.

What's left looks like
archipelagos or
ice bergers.
(Those are little ice bergs.)

I come down
using garden sticks as ski poles
take old cards off the fridge
tired of looking at
snowmen on white paper
put up a double page
from The New York Times,
Travel Section

"Seduced by Rio and
Learning Its Secrets,"
a full spread of bronzed women
and men on the beach at Ipanema

and I smile, looking at the spread.
I feel like I'm on the beach, too,
especially if I turn the heat up.

I won't need to have angst
about airport security
or the actual flight
or perfumes or cigarette smoke
or the landing
or fumbling for my few words
in that gorgeous language:
Portugese.

I won't have to discuss
Yanqui foreign policy
with Brazilians or anyone

or worry how I look
in a one-piece bathing suit
amid so many bikinis
and trouble about varicose veins
that swelled with motherhood
and have not left.

NO.
I mean, YES.

I can be a girl at Ipanema

in this house
in this cabin

all a fever.

On the Train

Past Toledo, winter light glows
on remains of crops in the snow
blurring by our car.

I hear our coach attendant tell a
white couple from Minnesota
about Josephine Baker --
she gathered information
for the Resistance in France
during WW II -- she helped a
Jewish former husband and
friends escape the Nazis.

They never heard of Josephine
Baker.

She left Jim Crow in the U.S.
came to live in Paris and
danced bare breasted: Paris style.
Jo Bouillon, her husband, said
she was the best dressed naked
woman in the world. (She clothed
herself in six languages).

In the US, Winchell killed her
career. In Paris, soldiers fought
to carry her coffin.
Josephine Baker salud!

Black History Month on the train
where earth is a frosted valentine.

Borders

Grandson Jaden is rosy cheeked
but tired of sledding
and a chill rises in all of us.

We head for Sanchos Taquirias,
a cafe across the highway
from ever flowing Lake Tahoe.

Inside the cafe
a pale green froth of hot sauce
appears on my plate.

I push it onto the fish
delicately seasoned
with cilantro. We are in Mexico.

Of course, *it was Mexico*
before the war
and I think from the taste
this fish was smuggled across
the new border a century ago
coming home to greener waters

only to be fried
to accept the yoke of hot sauce
wrapped in tortillas

still burning my lips
lest I forget
this was Mexico.

Snowshoeing at Home

Snowshoeing
we two
over snow's two feet

past hemlocks
whose branches
sigh for the wind

down to the beloved lake
nebes

we read the stories of other tracks

squirrels, mice, fox
mikoa-ak, alezawak
wokwses

looking up
for the woodpecker
o'basas
drumming in the blue
above land

we catch the wafer
the pale wafer
of the moon.

Mud Season &
Spring

Opening the Doors

I open the doors
before dawn
to hear
the brook singing

See
even in the shadows
how sun
and gentle rain
have peeled
the crust of snow
from the soft belly
of my garden.

Day Breaks in Montpelier

Day breaks in the city
pungent with gas, exhaust, industry.

Monocultures of coffee & sugar
provide the fix, hurry all these bodies
into buses, cars and trucks.
Now all the puddles are flowing
on Prospect Street!

I wave good-bye to grandson, Joey
boarding his school bus
say Goodbye to son, Malcolm
after sharing miso soup.

From the second floor
of the dentists' office
I see SUN and shout so.

"Don't squint or it'll go away,"
the dentist's assistant says.
I won't squint and the sun doesn't go away.
IT SHINES.

Shines on bare maple and locust trees
now shines on Abenaki, Black and White
shines on Israel and Ishmael.
We could heal
throw lotsa matza meal to the heavens
no leaven   like confetti at a shero's parade.

Cancun Cantada

In the park of Jefes
of heroes of the Revolucion

Jorge sees like a rhyme
lizards crawling out
for the sun
one at a time.

Dark gray on gray rock.

I, too, with my dark and
cold scales clinging to hinder
drag up through the musty holes
of late winter

not meaning to mock
beating my feet against hard stone.

Squinting at the richness
of magenta tipped leaves
beads of sweat forming
in blue green sleeves.

With my cold blood in tow
I pay homage to Kinich Ahau
locked in the sweet embrace
                    of the sun.

The Day Before....at Pinon Draw

The winds sing today.
The winds sing in this forest of pines.

Pine cones dribble from one tree to another
on Earth's carpet of old needle designs.

Even sitting in a plastic chair
typing at an old machine
I feel wrapped in winds' song
on this mountain at Pinon Draw.

Though radio works in son Emile's truck
the economy does not work
and today or tomorrow
the empire's troops -- so many so young
themselves -- will invade
the already-bombed, hungry,
good-water-deprived and
medicine-needy country of Iraq
half the population
children under fifteen.

Everyone has a death song
if she knows it   if he knows it
                or not.

These winds sing
for the pines reaching towards spring
but also for the children
who were too young to learn a death song
and die and will die in this war
dicots uprooted from the garden of life.

Almost to Spring
the war erupting from a volcano
of greed for oil
burns hot lava on the frogs
silences their songs.

(The songs I long for on rainy nights
echoing from the wetlands at home).

Here at Pinon Draw
with enough gas and oil in our tanks
to cook and drive
no bombs above
just cow pies below
we plow through the days
of winds' song

hoping for some way of redemption
when our voices
"NO War!" were ignored...

some blessing of the pines
who wave away remorse
with their soft needles
practicing Chi-gong in the breeze.

Seder

A gray dawn, light snow like crumbs
coats the bumpy driveway
and I am already tired

and still there is
soup to simmer
parsley and celery
onions, ginger and yams

and bricks and mortar
apples and cinnamon
to chop together
hinting at the insidious
                    sweet lure
in certain forms of slavery.

The mail arrives
the check from a dentist
who messed up my gums and teeth.

Celebrate.
Now we make love
not worry.

I feel Spring coursing
through your veins
as you will with love
shake me loose from winter.

And driving me
to Passover Seder
let this woman go.

Later, in the darkness
I take back memories of the seder
Anita's sweetness   her mercy
when I moaned
after mentioning *four plagues*....
as we spilled drops of grape juice
                    to diminish our joy.

"I don't remember any more plagues
and my glasses are broken
so I can't read this Haggadah."
And Anita couldn't read it either
and everyone else was silent
waiting on the word of the elders.

"I think," Anita said,
"Four is enough."

And the light in our grandson's eyes
when I spoke of Harriet Tubman
the Moses of her people
who brought every passenger from slavery
to freedom and never lost a woman or
a child or a man.

Looking up,
Joey asked: "Harriet Tubman...
Did she have brown skin?"

Yes.

May at Last

The road is silk
with rain

with hawthorn
blossoms
red.

The trees
the hills swell
with new
leaves.

A trillium
is
my gardenia

and you
are my garden.

Silver Mountain Sky

Silver mountain sky
Blow away my snows.
I feel so high
everybody knows.
The trees are rich with sugar
'fore the first green leaf appears.
Then a sea of green will shimmer.
Dance away. The sun is near.
Dance away. The sun is near.

Silver mountain sky
caressing firs and pines.
All the Earth is yours.
All the Earth is mine.
Now, the ground is swelling
soon with rainbow flowers
and the sparrow's telling:
Sing away. The song is ours.
Sing away. The song is ours.

Silver mountain sky
burn away the mist.
Every place I've laughed
Every place we've kissed.
Now I'm born again
red as any dawn.
Now the breeze's quiver
Floats on me. I am the river.
Floats on me. I am the river.
Floats on me. I am the river.

Music for **Silver Mountain Sky**

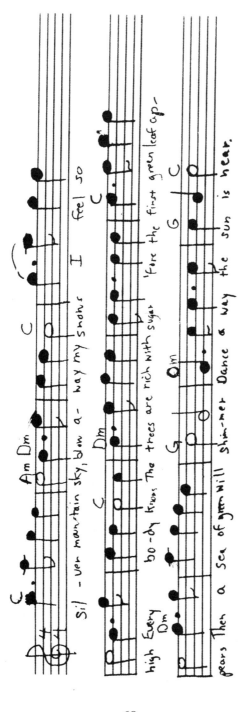

Lyrics and Music by
Phyllis R. Sawyer